Aches And Pains
by a Former Payne
Trusting God During Difficult Times

Kay Payne Galloway

Aches And Pains by a Former Payne: Trusting God During Difficult Times
ISBN: Softcover 978-1-951472-60-3
Copyright © 2020 by Kay Payne Galloway

All rights reserved. No part of this book may be reproduced or transmitted in any form or by any means, electronic or mechanical, including photocopying, recording, or by any information storage and retrieval system, without permission in writing from the publisher.

www.parsonsporch.com

*Aches And Pains
by a Former Payne*

Dedication

To: Ronnie, my wonderful husband. You have helped me through most of the things I have written about. You have been my helper, cook, laundry man, chauffeur, and took care of everything else I could not do. Thank you for everything you have done for me. Almost 42 years together, and I love you more than ever.

To: Jamie, Katie, and Jon, you are my life. All of you stepped up and helped as much as you could while working full time jobs and caring for my granddaughter, Maelyn Kay. You are the best! I love you all so much.

To: Maelyn Kay, you bring sunshine to my life every day. I love you with all my heart.

To: Karen, I don't know how I would have gotten through all of this without you. You have always been there for me since we first met many years ago. We have enjoyed life together during the good times and the bad. I think of you and your family as my family. Thank you for everything.

To: Cindy, Emily, Jennie, Shelia, Pam, and Debra, the best friends anybody could ever have. I thank you from the bottom of my heart for your prayers and for always checking on me. You all are the best and the funniest friends anywhere!

To: Ann Smith, I love you so much. God gave me a wonderful friend when I met you. You were such a blessing to me while we were in rehab. I treasure our friendship and can't wait till we can get together and laugh!

Foreword

by Karen Sanford Randolph

Sixty plus years ago in a hospital nursery in Tennessee, a friendship was born.

God gave me a special friend to share many of life's adventures with. One time we even shared fishing bait. My Papaw caught a spring lizard and cut it in two parts, Kay got the head, and we went off to the creek with our cane poles and shared bait. We caught us some "little" bluegill.

The stories that she writes about, many were quite scary at the time, all lead to a focus on where the strength comes from to endure.

Now, begin the life/health adventures of my dear friend, Kay.

Trust in the Lord with all thine heart... Proverbs 3:5-6
A friend loveth at all times. Proverbs 17:17A

Introduction

God is our refuge and strength, a very present help in trouble.
Psalm 46:1 NASB

I thought about writing a book when I was in therapy for a broken leg. One of my friends said that I have had so many things happen to me that I should put it all in a book. Well, I am not a writer. I never liked writing anything. When I had to write my master's thesis, I really thought I would never get through it; I did and made an A. That was many years ago, and I haven't written much of anything since, except lesson plans.

I was born in Oak Ridge, Tennessee, and we moved to Etowah, Tennessee, when I was just a baby. I was raised by wonderful Christian parents and had wonderful grandparents. We were a family of four including my older sister.

My sister, Judy, and I were very different. She was outgoing, and I was very shy. We were involved in several activities. We both were Brownies and Girl Scouts. We also took piano lessons. She was good at listening to music and playing it on the piano, but I had to have the music in front of me. Whenever Judy would get a new piece of music to learn, she would bring it home and let mama play it for her. She would sit down and play it without ever learning the notes.

Mama finally caught on and quit playing her music so she would learn the notes. It didn't work. She took lessons for a while longer and then quit. I continued on through college.

We also had all those lovely childhood illnesses- measles, mumps, and chicken pox. There were no vaccines at that time. My poor mama and grandma usually had two or more weeks of one child and then the other sick with each of these diseases. I especially remember chicken pox. I stayed with my grandma and she believed in Calamine lotion for the itch. To this day, I cannot stand the smell of Calamine lotion. It was also Bible School time at church, and I couldn't go but Judy could. I was so disappointed. I also remember when we had the mumps. My dad was working in Morristown and would come home on the weekends. Several weekends he came home to the new disease of the week. Needless to say, we survived those diseases, and I am so glad there is now a vaccine for the little ones.

When I was in the Girl Scouts, we went on a picnic at Quinn Springs, across the road from the Hiwassee River. We always had a fun time and we had great leaders that took us camping and places to work on our badges. We were jumping around on some big rocks, and for some reason I fell or passed out. One of our leaders, a registered nurse, came over to check on me. I had no pulse. I guess she thought I was dead. I don't know what happened after that, but I came to, because I am still here. I did not remember the incident, but my mama told me about it later.

The following are several things that have happened to me through the years and how I have overcome these obstacles with a lot of family support and a lot of prayer

Childhood Memories

Children, obey your parents in the Lord, for this is right. Honor your Father and Mother, so that it may be well with you, and that you may live long on the earth. Ephesians 6:1-2 NASB

I had a wonderful childhood. My mom and dad were great parents and I had my Grandma and Grandpa Quintrell and Granny Payne. My mom and dad worked, so growing up my sister and I stayed with our grandma and grandpa during the summer. They just lived two streets over from us. We had a great time. They would take us on trips to the mountains, on picnics, and we would visit relatives. My mom was an only child, but my grandpa's brother had 22 children, so we had a lot of relatives.

My grandpa worked on the railroad, and my grandma was constantly doing something around the house. She always stayed busy. Once a day she would tell us to play in the living room and she would lay down for about 15 or 20 minutes and take a short nap. I guess that energized her because she would get up ready to get busy again. My grandpa was known for his carved walking canes. He would take a piece of cedar and carve a cane and then make a little cage with a ball in it. He would then put two pegs in a hole. The pegs were bigger on both ends than the hole. He would never tell us how he got those pegs in the hole. Everybody would ask but he still wouldn't tell. When he was in his late 80s, he finally told me. I have never told anyone, but I guess I will eventually tell both my daughters. He sold a lot of those canes, and they are all over the world.

My grandma and grandpa were very frugal. Grandma would go shopping at the Salvation Army Store and then show us the "new" shirt she bought for 25 cents. Grandpa would go buy a car when he needed a new one, and he always paid cash! Nothing was bought on credit. They didn't even have a checkbook. They were not rich; they just didn't think they needed a lot of stuff. Grandma would always cook our birthday lunch and when you got through eating, you could look under your plate and find money. When I was in college, Grandma would call me and tell me to come by her house as I was going to school. She had gotten up early in the morning and made me a bag of homemade fried peach pies. Did I share? I don't think so! To say that I was spoiled is an understatement.

We visited with Granny Payne a lot. She just lived about four miles south of us in the big city of Delano. Delano did not have a traffic light or any stores. It did have a gas station and post office. We always had Thanksgiving dinner and Christmas dinner at her house with the whole family. My dad had two brothers and two sisters, and they all had children. The house was full of people. I guess Granny was used to a house full of people because she was one of 18 children in her family. We have a lot of relatives on my dad's side, too. There were always a few extra that showed up at Thanksgiving and Christmas. Everyone brought food and we had a lot to eat. I remember the men always ate at the kitchen table, the kids ate in the next room and the moms ate wherever. Granny made the best homemade rolls to go along with all her other wonderful dishes.

There was always a lot of kids to play with when we were altogether. I remember playing outside on a Sunday afternoon at Granny's and a bunch of us were running around the house. Everyone turned around to go the other direction except one person. He was just tall enough that his head hit my eye. I got to go to church that evening with a nice black eye!

Having wonderful parents and grandparents is a blessing. I miss them all so much, but I have wonderful memories.

Best Of Friends

A friend loves at all times. Proverbs 17:17 NASB

My best friend was Karen. We met each other when she was three days old. I was nine months old. We did everything together. If I wasn't at her house, she was at mine. Her parents and my parents were the best of friends. Karen and I started school together and went through our second year of college together. When we started our junior year of college she went to the University of Tennessee (Go Vols). I went to college closer to home at Tennessee Wesleyan College (Go Bulldogs). This was the first time we had ever lived that many miles away from each other.

Some of my favorite memories were her dad picking us up from elementary school in a horse and buggy. We thought we were something. He also let us, or actually told us, to help haul hay. Karen and I would pick up the bales of hay and put them on the truck. Her brother drove the truck. We didn't think that was quite right, but in all fairness, Karen and I couldn't drive. We worked rather cheap with our payment being an ice cream cone. Her mom took us to Michigan to visit relatives, and to Mississippi to visit her brother in the Army. My mom took us to Illinois to visit family. Our dads would take us to the lake to swim. We had a lot of fun growing up and we still do. We are still best friends and she has been with me through all the crazy things that have happened to me.

Education, Marriage, Babies, And Surgery

For we are His workmanship, created in Christ Jesus for good works, which God prepared beforehand so that we would walk in them. Ephesians 2:10 NASB

As the years went by, I went on to college majoring in music education. I had studied piano for many years. I graduated from Tennessee Wesleyan College (now University) in 1976. I worked for several years in the office of a manufacturing plant. There were no music positions open in the area, so I played the organ for church and taught piano lessons.

I married Ronnie Galloway, the love of my life, on August 19, 1978. Little did he know that his wife was going to have lots of problems. Bless his heart. We had known each other for years but didn't date until 1973. On our first date we went to see John Wayne in "Big Jake". Several years ago, I found a DVD of "Big Jake" and bought it for Ronnie for our anniversary. We have been married for almost 42 years.

Before Ronnie and I were married, we had found a little house to rent. When we started to move things in, a bigger house was for sale. We bought the house and never did live in the rental. We were now homeowners. It was a very little house in town with two bedrooms and one bathroom. It was indeed a fixer upper. We put cabinets in the kitchen and worked on the bathroom. Every so often we would call our good friends Mike and Debbie and ask them if they would want to come up for supper. Mike would always say "Is the sewer line stopped up again?" Indeed, it was! Ronnie and Mike would work on unclogging the sewer line and it would be ok until the next time the roots got in it. My grandpa and grandma paid off the loan on our house and SUV. What a relief that was. We were both working but did not make a lot of money, and grandpa asked me what we owed on the house. I told him and he said to meet him at the bank. We had never asked for help paying our bills, but we were thrilled when he said they wanted to help.

In 1981, we decided it was time to add to our family. We were both very happy when we found out we were pregnant. Our baby was due on January 2, 1982. Two weeks after my due date, our baby decided it was time to enter the world. My water broke at home early in the morning. It was a terrible winter with ice and snow everywhere. Thank goodness we had a four-wheel drive vehicle. When we got to the hospital, I wasn't having any pain and I thought "this is easy". What did I know!? Labor pains started around lunchtime. Oh my, was I wrong about that easy stuff! The doctor's office was closed that day because of the weather, so my doctor was at the hospital most of the day. He would come in and sit and talk to Ronnie about cars, cameras, and everything else. I wanted to scream shut up, I'm in pain here! The doctor always told me that they don't call it labor for nothing. A friend of ours worked in the operating room and brought me a poster of Tom Selleck that they had in the nurse's locker room. She hung it on the wall to use as a focal point while I was doing my breathing during labor. He was great to look at, but after a while, I didn't care who I was looking at. I just wanted this baby out. It wasn't a long labor, thank goodness. Jamie Erin Galloway made her appearance at 5:39 p.m. on January 15 weighing 7 lbs. 2 oz. Thirteen days late, but we were thrilled.

With the weather being so bad, I didn't have many visitors except immediate family. The hospital lost power and the nurses would come through the hall and tell us that breakfast would be late because the power was out. We headed home a couple of days later and had a flat tire on the way home. Thankfully, we were still close to the hospital when that happened, and we stopped to get it fixed. I sat in the car with my new baby while they fixed the tire.

Ronnie, who taught high school biology, was out of school for two weeks because of the weather. That was rather nice because he could bond with the baby and help me around the house.

When Jamie was almost 3 years old, we were awakened by the fire alarm on Christmas Day. We had a floor furnace and it was cherry red. The thermostat had messed up and the furnace was staying on. We didn't think anything was on fire yet, but we needed it checked. Ronnie called the fire department and I went to get Jamie. The furnace was between her room and ours. I was scared to death. Santa Claus had been there, and I didn't want her to get up to see firemen in our house. I stayed in her room with her next to the front door until everything was checked out. There ended up being no fire, but we couldn't leave the furnace on. We replaced the furnace and spent another year in our little house.

During the last pregnancy we were building a house. Our little home had served its purpose, but we needed more room. My dad owned the land next to Granny's house and he gave us two acres to build our house. Ronnie found out real fast that you don't build a house when your wife is pregnant. He said I fired some workers that were just standing around doing nothing. I don't remember that, but I probably did fire them. It was a busy time taking care of a three-year-old, working a full-time job, and trying to find time to pick out fixtures for the new house.

In November 1985, we were blessed with another child. My labor started at home and we went to the hospital that evening. They checked everything and said it will be a while, so they were going to send me home with a sleeping pill. I told them that I was not going home that I was here to have this baby. This one was eight days late. They let me stay a little while longer and the nurse came in to check everything and said she was glad I didn't go home. Labor was once again horrible. I don't know why I thought I didn't need an epidural. I also didn't have Tom Selleck to look at this time. I told Ronnie that if we ever have another child, I want drugs. On November 21, 1985, Kathryn Lynn "Katie" Galloway arrived at 3:43 in the morning weighing 7 lbs. 9 oz. When the doctor got her out, he held her up and said, "It's a squatter." We were now a family of four.

We moved into our new house three days before Christmas, 1985. Ronnie decided he would cut down a Christmas tree for us, and he ventured out to get one. We have a 10-foot ceiling in our living room and the tree was too tall. He took it outside and cut it off some and brought it back in. If my memory is correct, he had to cut it a third time. Finally, we had a tree, a new house, and a beautiful new baby.

I had gone back to school in 1980 and added elementary education to my teaching certificate. I got a job in 1988 with Etowah City School teaching 3rd grade. During my time at Etowah City I taught 3rd grade, 4th grade, and back to 3rd grade.

My first year with third graders was fun. I had a good group of kids. It was during the school year that I discovered a lump in my left breast. I went to my doctor and he sent me on to a surgeon. This was my first surgery, and I was scared to death. The doctor removed the lump and thank goodness it was benign. They taped me up from my shoulder to almost my waist. I was supposed to take the bandage off in three days. Well, three days passed, and Ronnie pulled it off. Oh, my goodness! I was allergic to the tape. It felt like I had a million pins sticking in me. I called the doctor and he said to get some mercurochrome that it would help dry it up. If you have ever used it, you know that it is ORANGE!!! Most of my chest was orange for several days. I am so glad no one could see it.

Fourth grade was also a good year. I was asked to take part in a volleyball game, teachers against the eighth graders. I said I would, and we were in the gym. One of the teachers hit me the ball during practice and my foot stuck to the floor and my knee went to the outside of my leg. Down to the floor I went. I knew what I had done, and I did not look at my leg. I took my hand and slapped my knee back where it belonged, got up and walked up to the office. Needless to say, my students had a lovely tale to talk about at home. My leg bruised from my hip to my ankle. I saw an orthopedic surgeon and he kept saying I didn't dislocate my knee, that doesn't happen to people our age. I told him that yes, I did dislocate my knee. He did arthroscopic surgery to make sure there were no tears, cleaned it up and finally agreed that yes, I did dislocate my knee. All I could say was "I told you so."

Aches and Pains

My last year at Etowah City wasn't as eventful health wise, thank goodness. I did have a couple of students that spoke Spanish. One had been there for a year, so she had picked up English quite quickly. The boy who came to my class that school year spoke no English. He was very sweet and worked on learning English. I had labeled everything in the room in English and we had another teacher, Anna, at the school that spoke Spanish. If I needed to tell him something, I would take him to her, and she would tell him whatever I needed her to tell him. Parent/Teacher conferences were also fun. His mom spoke no English so she would talk to his dad and his dad would talk to me. I would talk to his dad, and he would talk to his mom. It was an interesting year. When this student was in 8th grade he came back and thanked me for all the help I had given him. The whole class was a good, fun group of students. While teaching at Etowah City, I started classes to earn my Master's Degree in Education. I completed the courses and graduated in 1990.

During the summer I got a call from the principal at the high school. The principal was the same one I had as a student. When I answered the phone, he said this is Joe, Joe Quirk. All I could think was this is not Joe. He was always Mr. Quirk. Everyone respected this man so much. He called to see if I would be interested in teaching music at the high school. I interviewed with him, and he offered me the job. I told him I would talk it over with Ronnie and let him know. We discussed it and I took the job. Ronnie and I rarely saw each other at school. He was on one end of the building teaching biology, and I was on the other end of the building. We also drove separate vehicles most of the time. I drove a Chevy Trailblazer and always parked in the main parking lot. We had a very bad storm one morning with a lot of lightning. I could see the parking lot from my room and saw that the lights on my SUV were on and thought that is odd. I got my keys and tried to unlock my doors, but nothing worked. When the storm finally passed, I went to check on it and it was dead. Lightning had come in through the antenna and gone through the whole dashboard and went out the front tire and busted a hole in the concrete. I watched the news that night and saw my vehicle on a tow truck going out the school gate. That lightning bolt caused almost $6,000 worth of damage.

We both had a great time working at Central. Ronnie taught at Central High School of McMinn County for 34 years. I was there for 27 years. We made many great memories.

Living With Dizziness

The spirit of a man can endure his sickness, but as for a broken spirit who can bear it? Proverbs 18:14 NASB

You know that saying "If it is going to happen, it will happen to me", well it is true. I seem to always have something weird happening.

When I was about 10 or 12 years old, I got up and was walking to my bedroom. I walked into the door facing. I was so dizzy I could not stand up. I yelled for mama, and she got me to lay down. That helped, and I wasn't so sick. If you have ever had vertigo, you know what I mean. It is a miserable thing to have. The doctors did not really know what was going on, so they tried different medicines to try and control it. I would never know when it was going to happen.

I was on choir tour with my church group and we were in Maryland. We were staying in church members homes. Well, after riding so much, it hit. Dizziness and nausea and I didn't know what to do. I was rooming with my best friend Karen, and she knew what was happening. The people we were staying with got me to a bed, and it finally got better. While I was on that bed, I took out my contacts. Well, I got one in the case and thought I got the other one in the case but when I started to put them in the next morning, one was missing. Great, I was going to have to wear my glasses the whole choir tour. I went downstairs to the bed I had been on and there was a crocheted bedspread. I thought I would never find it. I looked down and there it was. Thank goodness. I think the people we were staying with had also slept in that bed.

I have suffered with it for many years. I eventually saw an Ear, Nose and Throat doctor who did some tests in his office and decided he needed some more extensive tests. Off to the hospital in Chattanooga I went. I spent about 3 days having tests run. EKG, EEG, blood work and several other things I don't remember what they are called. Ronnie and I were sitting in my room and I looked around and noticed there was not a faucet on the sink. We checked out other things in the room and decided I was in the mental health part of the hospital. Great, they think I am nuts. I can only hope they put me in that room because the hospital was full.

The doctor came by and said "well, you have a brain, but you don't have syphilis." He thought that was funny. He also said they could not find anything that was causing the vertigo and he thought it was anxiety. I never believed him. They gave me an antihistamine and motion sickness medicine and sent me home. I will get to what happens later in another section of the book.

Allergic To Everything

Peace I leave with you. My peace I give to you; not as the world gives do I give to you. Do not let your heart be troubled, nor let it be fearful. John 14:27 NASB

If you have ever suffered from seasonal allergies, you probably know the runny nose, itchy eyes, coughing and other things that happen. I have always had seasonal allergies, but my biggest problem is medicine allergies.

I was about 19 years old and had a terrible throat infection. The doctor gave me an antibiotic and I started taking it. I got a little itchy and started having a rash. I went back to the doctor and he said that I had the measles. Well I had already had the measles, but I guessed there must be another type. I kept taking the antibiotic. By the next morning I looked like something out of a horror movie. It was a Saturday, so mom called the doctors nurse who was a good friend of ours. She came to the house and said stop the medicine, it is not measles.

The itch was the most horrible thing I had ever been through. I couldn't sleep. I played solitaire all night and scratched. I know my mom and dad got tired of hearing me shuffle cards. Sometimes I would doze off and my mother would come in and ask if I was ok. I finally told her to just check to see if I was breathing and let me sleep. The medicine I was allergic to was making me swell up and the capillaries in my legs burst and my legs turned purple. It took more than a month to recover from this allergic reaction.

My second bad allergic reaction was after I was married. My daughter and I were both sick and went to the doctor. He gave us both some medicine. Well, I was allergic, again. I had a really bad rash and horrible itching. I didn't sleep for days. Ronnie took me back to the doctor and I grabbed him by the shirt and screamed "I haven't slept in three days." He looked a little shocked that some crazy woman was screaming at him. He gave me something to make me sleep. Finally, some rest!

The latest allergies have been with diabetes medicines. I was on a really good medicine to control my Type 2 diabetes, but the price of this medicine went from $47 a month to $479 a month with insurance. I thought that was a bit pricey! The doctor changed my medicine to a cheaper one and of course I was allergic. I tried two more, and I was allergic to them, too. We are now looking for something else that is not going to cost a fortune. I am one of those people that if I don't like something or have a problem with something, I write letters. I wrote the President of the United States, my Representative, and my Senator about drug pricing. I heard back from all of them. I also sent emails to the drug company. I never did get a reply from them.

I have had several more reactions to medicine through the years. Even though they were miserable, thank goodness they were all skin reactions and not breathing problems.

Every time I give my list of allergies to the nurse when I am admitted to the hospital, they just shake their head and say, "That sure is a long list. What can you take?"

Dealing With Anxiety

Trust in the LORD with all your heart and do not lean on your own understanding. In all your ways acknowledge Him, and He will make your paths straight. Proverbs 3:5-6 NASB

In 1990, I lost my wonderful grandpa. He was 90 years old and had always been in good health. He had a stroke and I was devastated. He died shortly after he had the stroke.

In 1992, my dad was sick and was hospitalized at our local hospital with a blood clot in his leg. We got a call from the hospital that he was roaming the hall and didn't really know where he was. They moved him to ICU because his breathing wasn't good, and he started seeing things that were not there. My sister and I would have to beat ants off the wall that he thought were there. The doctor had him transferred to the University of Tennessee Medical Center in Knoxville. They immediately put him in ICU and worked to keep him alive. They ran every kind of test trying to find the problem. Nothing showed up. The doctor suspected non-Hodgkin's lymphoma. Dad was in ICU for about 7 days and we had to make the decision to let him go. I can honestly say, it was the worse day of my life. My precious dad died. He was only 70 years old.

My mama requested an autopsy because she wanted to know what happened. It took about two months for us to finally find out what had caused his death. It was non-Hodgkin's lymphoma and was in almost every part of his body. He was my hero. He was a WWII veteran serving in the 82nd Airborne. He was a deacon at our church and was an overall great man. I miss him so much.

I had a very hard time dealing with the loss of my grandpa and my dad. By 1994, everything came crashing down. I had just arrived at school and was in my office when my niece, Brandi, walked by. She looked at me and asked what was wrong. I was shaking and couldn't breathe. My heart was racing, and I thought I would have to be carried out of there. Brandi ran and got Ronnie and he took me to the hospital. They kept me at the hospital for a little while to rule out certain things and then gave me the diagnosis: Panic Attack!

I went to the doctor's office several days later, and he said he wanted me to see a psychiatrist in Cleveland. Oh great, I am nuts! I don't think I had ever heard of panic attacks. Well, that was a very eye-opening appointment. I had been holding everything in for so long that it all came out at once. I went home with medicine to help control the attacks. I don't know how many tears I shed or how many prayers I said.

I would wake up every morning shaking, and Ronnie would get my medicine to calm me down. My mama would come down and stay with me while Ronnie went to work. I would try to go out to eat with my family, but I would end up going outside and sitting in the car while they finished their meal. I could just feel the walls closing in on me and I could not stand being in a crowd. It took about 3 weeks for the medicine to kick in, and I was finally feeling better.

I started this book with the scripture from Psalm 46:1 *God is our refuge and strength, a present help in trouble.* I was lying in bed looking at a magazine one night, and I put it in the floor next to the bed and went to sleep. When I got up the next morning, I looked down and that verse was the first thing I saw on the cover of the magazine. I knew God was going to get me through this.

I have been on medication for years. I really didn't want people to know about it but now I don't care to tell people about what happened. If it helps someone, that is great. The psychiatrist said that if I knew how many people out there that were dealing with this that I shouldn't worry about it. I have talked to others that have dealt with panic attacks and hope I have helped them in some way.

Therefore humble yourselves under the mighty hand of God, that He may exalt you at the proper time, casting all your anxiety on Him, because He cares for you. 1 Peter 5: 6-7 NASB

Jamie Has Surgery

Behold, children are a gift of the Lord. The fruit of the womb is a reward. Psalms 127: 3 NASB

Jamie was a sophomore in high school when we discovered she had scoliosis, curvature of the spine. We knew what was going to happen, but you never want your child to have to go through a major surgery.

We took her to a pediatric surgeon in Knoxville. He ordered x-rays and showed us what was going on. I just stood there and cried. The doctor would say "mama, are you alright?" My child was going to have surgery, no I was not alright.

Surgery was scheduled and we got up early on surgery day and took her to Children's Hospital in Knoxville. They got her ready and Ronnie and I kissed her and just stood there and cried. We tried not to let her see us crying. We didn't want her to be afraid. Karen had come to Knoxville to be with us and our friend Bill was also there.

We prayed for our beautiful daughter. It was probably harder on me and her dad than it was for her. The surgery was successful, and she was in ICU for a little while. She was moved to a room and I was going to stay with her. She was feeling pretty good. They gave her morphine for the pain and just shortly after that she developed a horrible headache. She could not stand anyone talking, the tv on, or basically any kind of noise. The doctor came by to see her and we told him she was having horrible headaches. They finally decided it was the morphine. He changed her pain medicine, and everything got better.

Jamie did great with the surgery. She got to go home a day early. They had put electrodes on her head, and I was the one that got to try and get all the gooey stuff out of her long blonde hair. I combed and picked at her hair for a while.

Jamie came home after three days in the hospital and was on homebound to keep up with her schoolwork until after Christmas. She was not allowed to bend at the waist for three months. I accused her of throwing everything in the floor just so I would have to pick it up. She was a bit upset that she would not be able to get her driver's license when she turned 16. Her birthday is in January, so she was not able to drive after her surgery.

It is hard for parents to watch their child go through difficult things, but God is good. He was there with us the whole time and continues to bless us.

Working With Numb Hands

Long life is in her right hand; in her left hand are riches and honor. Proverbs 3:16

The year 2000 was a big year for us. Jamie was graduating from high school, we both had her in class, and she would be starting college. Katie was just about to start high school. I didn't know how I was going to handle my oldest daughter moving to Knoxville. Thank goodness for cell phones.

I was having problems with both my hands falling asleep. I couldn't hold a book without them being tingly and I was miserable at night. I would wake up in the morning with both my hands numb. I eventually went to a hand doctor in Knoxville and he did carpel tunnel release surgery on my left hand. Everything went well, and I was bandaged and in a sling for a few days.

I had ordered a piece of glass for a table from a place in Athens and Jamie said she would take me there to get it. We picked up the glass and started home. We were on a highway going about 55 mph and a man pulled out in front of us. Jamie slammed on the brakes and swerved to try and go behind him, but we didn't have enough room. We hit the car in the back door behind the driver and it turned around to the other side of the road. If she had not swerved, we would have probably killed the man in the car. When everything finally stopped, Jamie was screaming, and I was trying to get her to calm down and tell me if she was hurt. The airbags had deployed and burned her hand and we both had seatbelt marks. My knee had hit the dash and left an imprint of something on my knee. The piece of glass I had just bought fell in the floor and never broke. I also had a large glass of tea in my hand and I have no idea what happened to it. The sheriff's department, highway patrol and ambulance arrived at the scene and checked everybody out.

Poor Jamie was so upset about her cute little red Honda Civic, her first car. It was totaled. I told her what my dad always told me. Don't worry about the car, it can be replaced, you can't be replaced. The highway patrol officer told Jamie that she did a good job trying to avoid hitting the other car.

I couldn't get Ronnie on the phone, but I knew where he was. The only person I could think of to call that could get to him was Karen's mom, Dot. She found him and he showed up at the scene. I think he was a bit shaken.

The ambulance took us all to the hospital and had us checked out. Everybody was okay considering we just totaled a car.

Shortly after the wreck I did have to have arthroscopic surgery on my knee to see what had happened in the wreck to cause the pain. The doctor fixed it up and I was okay.

In 2001, I had the other hand worked on. It was my right hand this time and I am right-handed. Oh, what fun that was.

Figure 1. Granny Payne

Figure 2. Grandma Quintrell

Figure 3. Friends Lunch

Figure 4. Buddy

Figure 3. Getting into the house via tractor

Figure 4. Grandpa Quintrell with one of his walking sticks

Figure 5. Jamie and Maelyn

Figure 6. Jon, Maelyn, and Katie

Figure 7. Karen and Kay

Figure 8. Katie and Jon

Figure 9. Maelyn and Ronnie, also known as Papa

Figure 10. Kay and Karen's mother, Dot, at her 95th birthday

Figure 11. Ronnie and Kay on their trip to Alaska

Figure 12. Maelyn, age 3

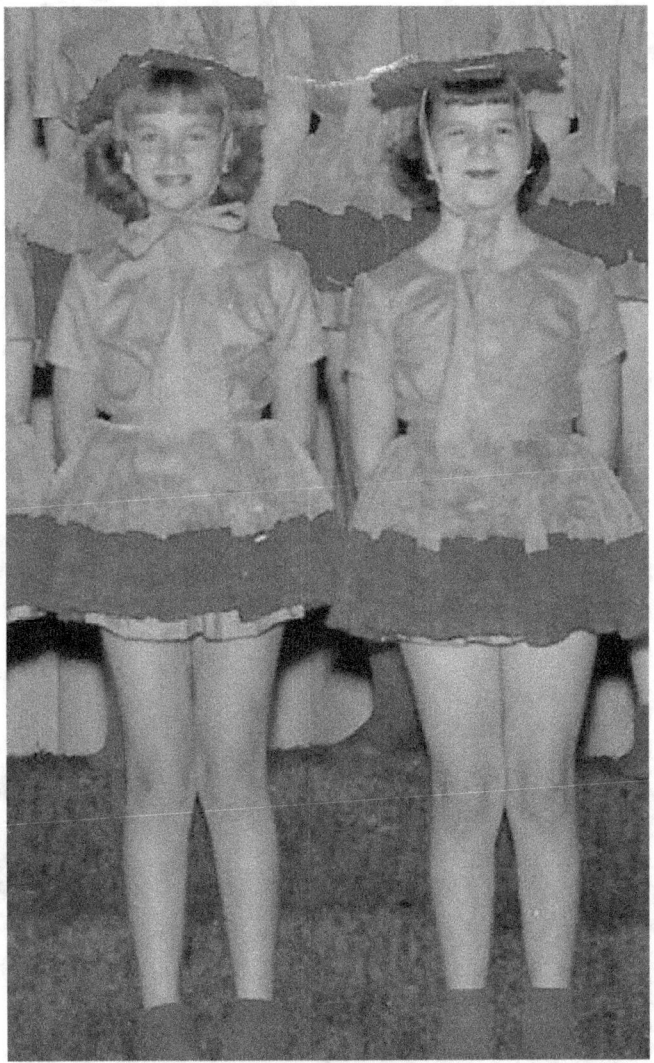

Figure 13. Kay and Karen dressed as marigolds in a play in elementary school

Figure 14. Kay, age 4

Figure 15. Kay, age 18

Figure 16. My Dad, Corporal Paul Payne, World II Veteran Paratrooper

Figure 17. Kay's Daughters, Katie and Jamie

Figure 18. Kay's mother and father

Figure 19. Kay's sister, Judy

Figure 20. Kay and Ronnie's wedding

Figure 21. Ronnie and Kay at a doctor's visit during the 2020 pandemic

Figure 22. Ronnie and Kay, 1978

Figure 23. Ronnie's favorite hobby.

Losing Loved Ones

For God so loved the world, that He gave His only begotten Son, that whosoever believeth in Him should not perish, but have everlasting life. John 3:16 NASB

He heals the brokenhearted and binds up their wounds. Psalm 147:3 NASB

Losing a family member is always a very hard time for those that loved them. My mother was a very happy person. She loved people and especially seeing old friends and relatives that she hadn't seen in a long time.

In the summer of 1995, I called to check on her and she didn't answer. I thought she was probably out somewhere. I usually talked to her every day. I waited a while and called again. No answer. I told Ronnie that I was going to go up to her house and make sure she was okay. He said he would ride up there with me. When we got there, I opened the door and didn't see her in the living room, so I yelled for her. I heard her but couldn't understand what she said. I went to her bedroom and she was in the floor with a big knot on her head and she couldn't get up. Her neighbor, a registered nurse, came over and said she thought it was a stroke. Ronnie called an ambulance and we got her to the hospital. The doctor came in and checked her and said she has had a stroke. That was not what I wanted to hear.

She was stabilized at the hospital and they sent her on to Chattanooga for rehab. Mom was paralyzed on her left side. She could talk to us but had a hard time eating. They worked her hard in rehab and she eventually was able to walk some. When she finally got to come home, my sister and her kids, Brandi, Brooke, and Jeramie, moved in with mom to help take care of her.

They all eventually moved to Judy's house. I had to take mom to the doctor, and I was by myself. We got in and out of the doctor's office fine but when we got home, I was helping her up the ramp and she lost her balance and we both hit the ground. I was yelling, "are you ok?" about a dozen times. We were both fine. I ran next door to Roy and Mary's house and told them I had dropped my mom on the ground. Roy came over and helped me get her up and in the house. We laughed about it later but at the time I thought I had really hurt my mom.

We eventually had to make the difficult decision to place mom in a nursing home. She lost her ability to walk and wasn't able to do much. We could not take care of her and needed some help.

In the meantime, my sister, Judy, was having health problems because of diabetes. She wasn't controlling her diabetes like she should, and it was taking a toll on her whole body. She was in the hospital and called me from the hospital and asked if Ronnie would sing for her funeral. I just sat down and cried. The doctors had told her there wasn't anything else they could do. She wanted to come home, so she went to her daughter's house and I went to see her there. I never got to talk to her. The next day I received a phone call early that morning that she was gone. This was March, 2005. She was just 52 years old. I couldn't believe it. We had to tell mom and I wasn't sure I could. Judy's girls, Brandi and Brooke, went to the nursing home with me, and Brandi told her mamaw. We were able to take mom to the funeral home before anyone was there. An aide from the nursing home came with us to help.

In May 2006, I was at school and received a phone call from the hospital that mom was in the ICU. I left school as fast as I could and went to the hospital. She was very sick, and everything was shutting down. I stood in her room and just sobbed. I don't think I have ever cried that hard in my life. I stayed in the ICU waiting room for a few days and went back to see her when I could. They called me back to her room and said it won't be long. I held her hand and kissed her until she passed. She would have been 82 years old in June.

Our family had a lot of deaths during 2005 and 2006. I lost my sister, mom, my Uncle Jim, and cousins Gary and Leon. It was a rough two years. I do know where they all are though, and I will get to see them again. God is good and faithful. Remember, He sent His Son to earth to die for our sins and rise from the dead so that we might have eternal life.

Can't Eat, Oh No!

The righteous cry, and the Lord hears and delivers them out of all their troubles. Psalms 34:17 NASB

After my mom passed away, I had a lot to take care of. Going through all her things and trying to find a place for everything was a hard job. Ronnie and I had two storage buildings to clean out on a hot July day. It was miserable, but somehow, we got it done.

We went back to work in August 2006, and sometime in October I came home from work on a Friday and didn't feel well. I couldn't eat. I was miserable. I made it on crackers and water until Monday and saw the doctor. He put me in the hospital because I was dehydrated, and he wanted to run some tests.

On Tuesday morning the doctor came to my room and said that it was my gall bladder. It was working at about 15%. He asked me when I wanted it out. I said right now! He stood there a minute and said hold that thought. He left the room and the next thing he told me was that the surgeon could do it in about an hour. That was fast! I knew the surgeon and trusted him, so I called Ronnie at school. He got someone to watch his classes and he came to the hospital. That was the quickest scheduled surgery I had ever had.

That night I was sitting on the side of the bed hurting some and thinking about all the things that had happened recently. I looked up and in walked Karen's mother, Dot. I always called her my other mother. She had been visiting her husband, Curtis, who was in the nursing home rehab. She said that Curtis wanted her to come see me to make sure I was alright. How sweet is that! They have always been like my second parents and I love them very much. Curtis passed away not too long after my mother, but Dot is 95 years old and looks as beautiful as ever.

I went home the next day and was feeling better and was finally able to eat something.

Wedding Time

For this reason a man shall leave his father and mother, and be joined to his wife; and they shall become one flesh. Genesis 2:24 NASB

He who finds a wife finds a good thing and obtains favor from the Lord. Proverbs 18:22 NASB

In 2010, we were planning a wedding! Katie and Jon were getting married on July 31. What a busy time that was. They planned their wedding to take place at North Etowah Baptist Church, the same church where Ronnie and I were married.

Of course, if something is going on, I have some kind of medical problem. I had to have my foot operated on in August 2009. It was supposed to be a simple operation and I had to wear one of those lovely boots that you strap on. Well, stupid me, I went back to work and was getting my room ready for the beginning of the school year. I pushed the piano where I wanted it and put too much pressure on my foot. The next morning, I could not put my foot on the floor. It was very sore. That little small incision had to be opened back up five times. I was so tired of walking in that big black boot and I was determined to get out of it by wedding time.

We worked hard on the wedding plans and I must say that I thought it all turned out beautiful, except for my shoes. I had ordered a pair of really pretty sandals and they were dyed to match my dress, the most expensive dress I have ever owned. I couldn't wear them because of the incision. I ended up giving them to Jamie because they also matched her dress. I didn't have time to go buy another pair, so I wore a really ugly pair of sandals that I already had, and they didn't bother my foot. I just kept thinking; I hope nobody looks at my feet!

The wedding was wonderful, and Katie and Jon went on their honeymoon in Mexico. When they got back, they were planning on moving to Wake Forest, North Carolina for Jon to attend Southeastern Baptist Theological Seminary.

At the end of December, we all helped to pack them up and on January 1, 2011, it was like a caravan going to North Carolina. Ronnie was driving the big truck. Jamie and I were in our car loaded with stuff and Jon's parents, Jerry and Nancy, were also loaded down and in the caravan. We got them moved in while it was drizzling rain all day and tried to get things placed where they belonged the best we could.

Late that afternoon, Ronnie, Jamie and I said goodbye and headed back to Tennessee. We both had to be at church the next morning. He was the music director at Wetmore Baptist, and I played the piano at North Etowah Baptist. I cried like a baby when we left. All I could think of was that I was leaving my daughter in another state with some man! I cried most of the eight-hour trip home. Ronnie probably wanted to cry because he got stopped for speeding two times. Once in North Carolina and the second time in Tennessee about 5 minutes from our house. He didn't get a ticket for either one thank goodness. We probably scared the officers to death. Working in the rain had done nothing for my hair. It was huge and I had the really ugly cries. We got home about 1:30 in the morning and got up the next morning and went to church. There's nothing like an eight-hour drive to North Carolina and an eight-hour drive back to Tennessee in one day. We were exhausted.

Katie and Jon lived in Wake Forest for six years and our granddaughter, Maelyn Kay, was born there. Jon finished school with a Master of Divinity degree. We are so proud of him. He got a job as Youth and Discipleship pastor at a church in Knoxville, Tennessee. They were closer to home!

Pain, Pain Go Away

Trust in the Lord forever, for in God the Lord, we have an everlasting Rock. Isaiah 26:4 NASB

Somehow, I knew my time was coming for some kind of joint replacement. My mother had both her knees replaced. Well, of course I had problems. The first thing to bother me was my right hip. It was sore but I just kept on going.

I held off as long as I could until it got to where my hip would lock up and I couldn't move, and the pain was so bad that I would just stand in place and cry. It got worse as the days went on. I got cortisone shots and took ibuprofen trying to get some relief.

I was walking with a cane and tried my best to stay at work. My planning period was the last period of the day. I was sitting at my desk and I stood up. The pain was so bad that I immediately picked up the phone and called the office and said if I can get to my car, I am going home. The office sent the school resource officer to my room to help and when my husband heard the intercom calling for the SRO, he came to my room. I also had the principal, assistant principal, and an aide in my room with me. I was hurting so bad and just literally sobbing. I also confess that I don't think my language was very nice either.

I eventually got an appointment with an orthopedic in Knoxville. He checked everything out and told me that I was a good candidate for how another physician in the office did hip replacements. I said I don't care who does it, just get me some relief. My hip was replaced from the front instead of the back. After surgery, the therapist came by my room and wanted me to walk 100 feet. I walked 600 feet. I would meet other patients in the hall, and they would say "we have already heard about you." I never had to go to rehab, I just walked with a walker at home.

Ronnie said he could see it in my face that the pain was gone the first time I stood up after surgery. Hallelujah! I went home the next day and did very well. I felt like a new person.

Years Of Friendship

Delight yourself in the Lord; And He will give you the desires of your heart. Psalms 37:4 NASB

Having wonderful friends is a great thing. Everybody needs people they can have a good time with. I am blessed with seven of the greatest friends, Karen, Cindy, Emily, Shelia, Jennie, Pam, and Debra. We all grew up together and went to the same church.

For the last several years we have been getting together, talking and laughing at the different things that happened to us through the years. We also talked about work, kids, and grandkids. Together we have all suffered through losing loved ones, illnesses, and other problems.

We got together one day and went to Pigeon Forge and spent the day learning how to make a basket. We also try to get together with some of our youth choir members from the 1970s and reminisce. Everyone brings a dish and we sit around and talk about how old we are now and what body part hurts.

The eight of us started having birthday parties when we all turned 60. We would take turns hosting the party for whichever one was turning 60. We always had great food and a lot of laughs. Six of us were or still are schoolteachers, one works in insurance and one works in assisted living.

We are a little more spread out now. Jennie moved to Virginia and Pam lives in Georgia. We still get together and sometimes some of our kids and grandkids show up, too. Our kids just look at us like we are a bit crazy, but that is okay, we probably are. We have a great time together.

My friends have been with me through a lot of the problems I have had. They have prayed for me and I feel so blessed to know these wonderful ladies.

Troubles With The Heart

I will lift up mine eyes unto the hills, from whence cometh my help. My help cometh from the Lord, which made heaven and earth. Psalms 121:1-2 KJV

Well, I thought 2012 was going to be a pretty good year after I had my hip replaced but I was wrong.

We went to church on a Sunday morning and we came home and ate lunch. I was sitting in the living room and I felt kind of weird. My heart was racing. Ronnie was in another room and I went in there and told him I think something is wrong. He checked my pulse and said it was very fast.

We went to our small hospital in town and checked in the ER. They took me on back and the doctor said you have afib or atrial fibrillation. They gave me several baby aspirin to chew up and poked a needle in my stomach with a blood thinner to prevent any blood clots. The doctor said he sees a lot of afib. I found out later that he was the local coroner.

I was put in ICU and given medicines to slow my heart down and get it back in rhythm. My regular doctor came by to see me daily and adjust whatever medicines that needed to be adjusted. My heart finally went back to a normal rhythm and I got to go home.

It happened again and they got in touch with a heart specialist in Knoxville and gave me a medicine he recommended. I had to stay in the hospital several days to make sure the medicine did what it was supposed to do. This time in ICU my next-door neighbor was from the jail. He screamed and cursed all night long. The nurses tried to calm him down and keep him in bed but didn't have much luck. The sheriff's department finally posted a deputy outside his room. I finally got some sleep. The next morning, he was gone. I asked where they took him, and they said the mental hospital.

I got so use to all the wires hooked to me that I would unhook them myself and yell out the door that "I'm not dead, I am just going to the bathroom." I would then get back in bed and hook myself back up.

The next time, I was in a regular room with a monitor on that the ICU nurses kept up with. They had given me the blood thinner again and of course I was allergic to it and turned red all over. It didn't itch, but I looked awful. I was there a couple of days and needed a bath. My room did not have a shower and they said I could go down toward the ER and use that shower. They removed all the monitors and off we went. Ronnie walked down the hall with me in a hospital gown looking like a red tomato. We get to the bathroom and I get ready to take a shower and it is broken, so Ronnie takes the hose off and holds it up to the sink and sprays me with water. It was so funny that we were laughing but I got my shower.

I was eventually sent to the heart doctor in Knoxville because nothing was keeping my heart in rhythm. He told me that I was a good candidate for a cardiac ablation. I had no idea what that was until he explained what he was going to do. I said that was fine, I am tired of having to go to the ER all the time because it always happened on a weekend.

I had the cardiac ablation and had to lay flat on my back for 10 hours. They don't want you to bleed out. My daughter, Jamie, would feed me a cheese sandwich and our friend Matthew would give me water trying not to pour it on me. After so long, I was miserable laying on my back and not moving, but there wasn't anything I could do. I spent one night in the hospital and went home the next day. I went back to work a couple days later. The ablation worked. I was so happy. My students all wanted to know what I had done so I told them that the doctor went in and burned part of my heart. I had heartburn. They thought that was awful! Afib is a very aggravating thing to have.

Four years later, in 2016 the afib came back. The doctor explained that when they go in the heart and laser the part that is causing the problem, that he can only go so deep. If he went too deep, I would end up with a hole in my heart. So, once again I was back at the hospital to have another ablation. Katie came from

North Carolina to stay with me. She had packed enough food for the whole cardiac floor. She was always asking me if I wanted a snack. She was pregnant at the time and didn't know.

The second ablation went well, and I was in bed for my 10 hours flat on my back. Fifteen and a half hours later the nurse finally came in to get me up. I sat on the side of the bed and the nurse said she wanted me to walk out to the hall. I got up and said I needed to stop in the bathroom. I got in the bathroom and sat down. In just a few seconds I was yelling for someone to get in there. I was sweating and thought I was going to pass out. Katie came running and got a cold wet washcloth to put on my head and the nurse was checking my sugar, my heart, and finally my blood pressure. My blood pressure would not register. All I could think of was that I was going to die like Elvis, sitting on the toilet! I don't think I would have made the news like Elvis. Katie kept wiping my face with a cold cloth and saying, "are you still with us mom?" I would weakly say yes. The nurse started an IV pumping fluid into me really fast and I started feeling better. You better believe we were all saying a prayer.

My heart doctor did put a small monitor (toothpick size) in my chest about a year after the ablation because I was still having a lot of flutters. It has about another year of battery life, but he has been pleased with how my heart is doing and I have very few flutters now.

How Am I Going To Get Through This?

Be anxious for nothing, but in everything by prayer and supplication with thanksgiving let your request be made known to God. And the peace of God, which surpasses all comprehension, will guard your hearts and your minds in Christ Jesus. Philippians 4:6-7 NASB

The 2017-2018 school year was going to be my last one. I had 30 years in education and Ronnie was already retired, so I decided that this was my last year. We wanted to travel some and spend more time with our family.

The beginning of 2018, I was having terrible pain in my right knee. Well, I knew what was coming, knee replacement. After x-rays, the doctor said both of my knees were worn out. He even said my kneecap was not in the right place. I told him that I had dislocated it several years ago and put it back in place myself. I guess I didn't get it in the right place. It was getting harder and harder to walk. New hip, bad knee. The doctor put a cortisone shot in my knee to give me some relief for a little while. It was a Wednesday and I went to church that night. I was sitting in prayer meeting and my heart decided to speed up. Prayer meeting was stopped, and everybody was concerned with what was happening. Someone went to get Brenda, a registered nurse, and she came over to see what was happening. I had three people standing next to me, the nurse, the pastor, and the mortician. Brenda told me when I call the doctor's office after hours line to make sure I ask which person I should leave with. I was hoping it wasn't going to be the mortician, even though he is a dear friend. Thank goodness it was not afib again. It was just the cortisone shot had made my heart speed up. It slowed down later and everything was good.

I took two weeks off from school and had a total knee replacement in April. I now know what my mother was talking about when she said it was terrible pain. The first time the therapist came in to get me up, I thought I was going to die. It was a Friday when I had the surgery and also Easter weekend. They were trying to get everybody done and out the door, so I came home the next day with pain medicine and orders to go to therapy in Etowah.

Ronnie and I had to figure out how to get me in and out of the house because we park in our basement and come up a whole flight of stairs. We decided the best way was in and out the utility room door at the other end of the house because there were only 5 steps and a handrail.

Therapy started, and it was horrible. I knew I had to do it and I did, but I also cried a lot! I kept apologizing but the therapist said not to worry that he had grown men that would cry. It didn't help the pain, but I felt better knowing I wasn't the only one who was blubbering like a baby.

On therapy days, Ronnie would take me. When he was working, Karen and her grandson, Fisher, would come get me. Fisher calls me Granny Kay, which I love! I told Karen that Ronnie is very picky with his yard so follow the tracks that are already in the yard. She did well.

Karen was taking me home from therapy one day and I was just sobbing. I told her that I would not wish this on my worst enemy. Then I stopped and said "well maybe one or two of them" if I have any enemies. I did have pain medicine which I took. It was an opioid and when the pain started getting better, I didn't want to take it much. The nurse told me to wean myself off of it. Well, I think I weaned a little too fast and I had the shakes, cries, and was basically a nervous wreck. I took Tylenol from then on.

I went back to school after two weeks with my walker and Tylenol and the knee continued to improve. I finished out the school year and said goodbye to my students and co-workers. Retirement here I come.

Pray without ceasing. 1 Thessalonians 5:17 KJV

North To Alaska

The Mighty One, God, the Lord, has spoken, and summoned the earth from the rising of the sun to its setting. Out of Zion, the perfection of beauty, God has shone forth. Psalms 50:1-2 NASB

Ronnie has always wanted to go to Alaska. He got busy and planned us a cruise with land excursions. Neither one of us had ever been on a commercial airplane or a cruise ship, so this was exciting.

I was still trying to get use to my new knee and was also having problems with my left hip. I saw the orthopedic and scheduled my hip replacement for when we got back from Alaska.

Going through the airport was a blast. Of course, with all the metal in me, I got to stand in the big scanner. We flew from Knoxville to Atlanta. This was the first time I had been in the Atlanta airport. Oh my, it is a big, busy place. The people working there were nice and saw that I was walking with a cane, so they got me a wheelchair. We had a long way to go to our gate. From Atlanta we flew to Vancouver, British Columbia. It is also a very busy airport.

We boarded our ship and found our room. We had a balcony room and it was wonderful. The first day on the cruise was a sailing day headed to Alaska. Ronnie and I took the time to wander around the ship and find out where everything was located. We were also hoping we wouldn't get seasick, and we didn't. We were on our balcony one afternoon and I had on a Tennessee t-shirt. Our neighbors next door saw my shirt and said they were from Oak Ridge, Tennessee. We also met a woman from Knoxville. It really is a small world.

We would get daily newsletters outside our door and we found out our Captain's last name was Galloway. How odd was that? We never did get to meet him, but we figured he was probably a cousin.

Alaska is absolutely beautiful. It was a very peaceful trip and the food was amazing. We got off the ship at different locations and shopped and did a tram ride, a train ride, and a glacier tour. Amazing sites to see. We would also try to call home while we were in port to make sure our family was alright.

I was determined my bad hip was not going to stop me from seeing everything I could see, so I just hobbled along and did pretty good.

We both did some shopping in the towns, and we shopped on the ship. The ship had a jewelry store and they had a necklace I really wanted. I did not want to pay the price they had on it. I would stop in everyday and check to see if it was any cheaper. No luck. I told them to look at me, I am on a cane and have to have surgery as soon as I get back and it would cost me a lot. The workers got to know me pretty well and would offer me a lower price and I kept telling them that it was too much. Finally, the last night we were on board I went to the jewelry store and I think they were tired of seeing me so they offered it to me and said this is the lowest price we can go. I bought it! It was a diamond whale tale necklace. The workers actually hugged me when I left. That was my biggest or I should say priciest purchase.

Of course, we had to get souvenirs for all the kids and a few friends. Then we had to worry about luggage weight. We got real creative packing our bags to go home.

We boarded our plane in Anchorage and headed to Dallas. When we got to Dallas, one of the workers said we could get put on standby for an earlier flight to Knoxville. We said that would be great and asked to make sure our luggage would be with us. They assured us that it would. We took the earlier flight and arrived in Knoxville and looked for our luggage. No luggage. It was put on our original flight which wouldn't arrive until around 5:30 p.m. Well guess where our car keys were? Of course, they were in the luggage.

We called Jamie and she came up to Knoxville and brought the extra set of keys. Ronnie went to get the car and it was dead. The battery had died while we were gone. Someone helped him get it started and we went to eat lunch because we hadn't eaten since dinner the day before. The car died again. Once again, a nice man stopped and helped to get it started. Jamie said she would just take it on home, and we could stay and wait on our luggage. She promised she would not stop anywhere on the way home. The luggage finally arrived, and we got to go home exhausted!

We hope to fly back to Alaska and just tour the state by car and see everything we can. It is such a beautiful state that I wish everyone could visit.

For the earth is the Lord's, and all it contains. 1 Corinthians 10:26 NASB

Benign Paroxysmal Positional Vertigo

These things I have spoken to you, so that in Me you may have peace. In the world you have tribulation, but take courage; I have overcome the world. John 16:33 NASB

Finally, 2018 was the year to find out what had caused all my dizziness through the years. Several months before we went to Alaska, I had terrible ear pain. I thought my head was going to explode. I called my doctor's office and spoke with the nurse. I was so upset and in a lot of pain. The doctor put me on some medicine and made me an appointment with an ear, nose and throat doctor. By that time, I had lost almost all the hearing in my left ear. He gave me a stronger medicine hoping it would help, but it didn't.

I eventually had to get a hearing aid and the doctor suspected it was Meniere's Disease and wanted me to see a specialist in Nashville. I told the Nashville doctor about all my dizziness through the years. He confirmed that it was more than likely Meniere's disease, but it was very hard to diagnose. He also told me that my hearing would not come back. My only option to get any hearing in that ear was a cochlear implant. Great, another surgery.

The one thing I did learn was that I could treat the dizziness by positioning my head certain ways and the tiny crystals in my ear would go back where they belonged. The crystals were the problem. They didn't want to stay in the right place. When they get out of position, the dizziness happens. Oh, how I wish I had known this years ago.

The end of July, after we got home from Alaska, I had a cochlear implant. I had to have it done before I turned 65 because Medicare would not cover the cost.

I had the surgery and went home the same day with a bowl on the side of my head to cover the wound. The doctor had told me that I would have a couple of days of dizziness. Oh no, not me. I had seven days of pure misery. I had to lay flat in the bed and hope I didn't throw up. I would hold on to Ronnie's shoulders and walk to the bathroom and then back to bed.

I sent an email to the doctor and asked when this would end and signed it "A Nauseated Patient." Finally, everything straightened up and I could walk without running into things.

The title of this section is Benign Paroxysmal Positional Vertigo. That is what I have. I still have problems if I lay on my left side or move too quickly but it is better than it used to be.

In August, I had to have the other hip replaced. It was done the same way as the first one, so I didn't have any problems and have done well.

Three surgeries in four months is not something I would ever want to repeat.

My First Broken Bone

The righteous cry, and the Lord hears and delivers them out of all their troubles. Psalms 34:17 NASB

After all the surgeries, 2019 had to be better. We had settled into a routine of just doing what we wanted to. Ronnie worked in the yard. I painted the kitchen and we were trying to fix things up at the house. We also loved visiting with our family and watching our granddaughter blossom into the cutest, funniest little girl.

We took a Sunday off and surprised Katie, Jon, and Maelyn at their church in Knoxville. Jamie went with us. It was May 5, Cinco de Mayo. We spent the afternoon together and had a great day.

We got home about 5:30 in the afternoon and changed clothes. We had left our little dog, Buddy, in the kitchen and we were gone longer than we thought we would be. He left us a puddle in the floor. We had both checked the kitchen and didn't see anything and we let him outside. I walked back in the kitchen and found it. My left leg went straight out and my right knee with the knee replacement went straight down to the floor very hard. I couldn't straighten my leg and I knew it was broken.

Ronnie heard me hit the floor and came in there and asked what he could do. I just said call an ambulance. He asked again what he could do. Again, I said to call an ambulance.

The ambulance arrived and I was lying in a puddle of dog pee with a broken leg. Ronnie tried to get as much pee out of the floor and off of me as possible. The EMT's were trying to figure out how to get me out of the kitchen. Because of the island in the kitchen, they could not get the stretcher in there. The fire department came to help. They splinted my leg the way it was bent and got what they called a scoop and scooped me out of the floor and took me to the ambulance. I was yelling at Ronnie to not kill the dog as I was being put in the ambulance. The EMT asked where I wanted to go, and I said UT Hospital in Knoxville. That is over an hour drive but that is where my orthopedic doctors are located.

I wasn't in a lot of pain unless I tried to bend my leg, so I just chatted with the man that was riding in the back of the ambulance with me. He told me about his wife and kids and that his kids were enrolled in a Baptist elementary school. We got to talking about church and he said he grew up Catholic and then left the Catholic faith and didn't go to church anywhere. He eventually went back to the Catholic church but decided that wasn't for him. He is now raising his family in the Baptist church. I told him that the best thing we did for our girls was to keep them in church and for him to keep his kids in church. He agreed. We chatted all the way to Knoxville.

I was taken into the ER and it was so full that my "room" was Hall B. I laid in Hall B for 9 1/2 hours just watching people come and go. They did take me for x-rays and gave me some pain medicine. After the morphine, I really didn't care where I was. Ronnie, Jamie, and Katie all got to the hospital and stayed with me for a while and our pastor came up and had prayer for me.

The next morning about 7:30 I was moved to pre-op. The anesthesiologist came by to see me and said he had seen me before. As many times as I had been up there, I'm sure he had seen me before. He told me he would be putting a tube down my throat after I was asleep. I told him that I had a lot of new, expensive dental work in my mouth and if he broke any, he would be buying them. He laughed and said he would try his best not to break any.

The surgery was over, and everything was put back together. The doctor, who is a trauma surgeon, did say that I had shattered my femur and it was one of the worse ones she had seen. Great, I really know how to do things really good.

I was in the hospital for four days and we made the decision that I should go to rehab in Farragut, just south of Knoxville. I was transferred by ambulance to rehab. I had asked for a private room, but they did not have any available at the time, but I would be on a list to get one.

I tried to get settled in and a nurse came in and asked me if I had eaten dinner. I said no and I thought she would probably bring me something, but she said everybody goes to the dining room for meals. No staying in bed there! She said to get in the wheelchair, and she would take me to the dining room. That would be fine except I was still in the hospital gown I arrived in and did not have a stitch of clothing on underneath the gown. Ronnie and Katie went with me and I kept telling them that I am not dressed for this. They kept saying don't worry about it, but I was sure several in there knew I was a new patient. I felt like people were looking at me. I was miserable sitting there in just my hospital gown, but I ate my dinner and went back to my room.

I finally got to talk to my roommate. She was the most wonderful person I could have roomed with. I know God put us together. We became fast friends. Her name is Ann and she had fallen and had a break in her hip. We discussed our injuries and families and got to know each other better. She has a daughter named Jamie and I do, too. We would lay in bed at night and tell stories and laugh. We would both say that we need to go to sleep and then one of us would say "but let me tell you about this." I know the other patients got tired of hearing us laughing.

Ann celebrated her 84th birthday on Mother's Day and I had Katie pick her up a present. She got her a bracelet and card. Her family came by and my family got to meet them. They are the sweetest people. Her husband is going through a rough time with dementia and we would talk about that. I hope in some way I helped her deal with what her husband was going through. I know she worried about him while she was in rehab. He is a very sweet person, too. She definitely helped me while being away from my family.

We both eventually got private rooms. She moved to a private room first and I really missed her even though she wasn't far away. I moved to a private room in another hall. It was a good distance from everything. My arms sure got a workout pushing myself in the wheelchair. Ann and I would sometimes be in therapy together, but we almost always had breakfast, lunch and dinner together. I would also play the piano that was in the sitting area and she would come out to listen.

Ann got to go home before I did, and I missed her so much. We still stay in touch and hope we can get together soon. While I am writing this, the country is in lockdown because of the corona virus so we can't get together, but we will as soon as we can.

I was probably at rehab another week after Ann left, for a total of three weeks. Before I went home, some wonderful men at church built a ramp up to my front door. Thanks to Stanley, Wayne, David, and Ronnie, I could now get in the house with my wheelchair. We did good using the ramp until it decided to rain and rain and rain. Our house is on a hill and we had to drive up the hill through the yard to get to the ramp. Ronnie got the SUV up the hill and we went somewhere. When we got back it would not go up the hill. It would just sit and spin in the mud. Well, I figured I would have to spend the night in the basement which doesn't have a bed or a bathroom. My creative husband came up with an idea. He went and got the tractor and put me in the front-end loader and took me up the hill. He did put a pillow in it for me to sit on. He had the wheelchair on the sidewalk, and he put me down next to it. Problem solved! We have since put in a stairlift to come in through the basement garage.

I went home trying to stay non weight bearing on my right leg. It's not as easy as it sounds. The doctor said I would probably be non-weight bearing for 3 months. Well, 3 months passed, and I still couldn't put my foot on the ground. I needed enough bone growth to hold all that metal in place and I didn't have any bone growth. I would go back to the doctor every six weeks to check for bone growth and the results were the same, no bone growth. I just burst out crying. About six months after the first surgery, I had to go back for a bone graft. I was also using a bone stimulator at home. Six weeks after the bone graft there was still no bone growth. I was devastated. The doctor said that the knee replacement was compromising the blood flow and the diabetes wasn't helping either.

I was determined to go back to church and play the piano after the first surgery. The doctor said it was okay to use the pedal on the piano with my broken leg, I just couldn't stand and put any weight on it. I love accompanying choirs and soloists. Our church has a lot of steps, and we had to figure out how to get me to the piano. Everything was worked out using ramps, and Ronnie just rolled me right in. I was glad to be back. I enjoy playing the piano so much. It is a good way to take your mind off of your problems. I have four pianos, four guitars, a banjo, mandolin, lap dulcimer, hammered dulcimer, bass guitar, and two ukuleles at my house. I guess I could forget about a lot of problems with music!

The decision was made to put me in outpatient therapy and try to put a little weight on my leg to stimulate blood flow. That is what I am doing right now, one year after I broke my leg. We are all praying this works. I hope I am walking good very soon.

What is next on my list of ailments? I don't know, but I do know who holds my future.

Final Thoughts

I did not write this book to just tell people all my problems. I wrote it to show that God is good, and He will see you through trials in life. I have been blessed with a praying family, praying friends and a praying church family. I don't know what I would have done without all of them. I also know that there is a purpose in everything that has happened to me. Maybe I have helped someone along the way. For that, I am thankful. I have tried to find the humor in some of the things that have happened to me. Sometimes a good laugh will just make you feel better. I have made it through some scary things, but I have always had God and my family there with me.

I hope that by reading this book you will grow closer to God. He is always there ready to listen to any troubles you may be having. If you don't know Jesus as your Savior, talk to someone about becoming a Christian. It is the best thing you could ever do for yourself.

Remember,

God is our refuge and strength, a very present help in trouble. Psalms 46:1 NASB

I can do all things through Christ who strengthens me. Philippians 4: 13 NASB

How blessed is he whose help is the God of Jacob, whose hope is in the Lord his God, who made heaven and earth, the sea and all that is in them; Who keeps faith forever; Who executes justice for the oppressed; who gives food to the hungry. The Lord sets the prisoners free. Psalms 146:5-7 NASB

www.ingramcontent.com/pod-product-compliance
Lightning Source LLC
Chambersburg PA
CBHW062039120526
44592CB00035B/1619